John Goodman

Long-Lost Chronicles of Solomon, and Poems

John Goodman

Long-Lost Chronicles of Solomon, and Poems

ISBN/EAN: 9783337318093

Printed in Europe, USA, Canada, Australia, Japan

Cover: Foto ©Thomas Meinert / pixelio.de

More available books at **www.hansebooks.com**

LONG-LOST

GHRONIGLES OF SOLOMON,

—AND—

⚜POEMS,⚜

—BY- -

JOHN GOODMAN.

DEDICATED TO ANN GOODMAN. MY WIFE.

CLEVELAND, O.

J. B SAVAGE, PRINTER, FRANKFORT STREET.

1884.

INDEX.

Chronicles of the Times of Solomon.

There have lately been discovered, since the English were in possession of Egypt, in one of the ancient tombs, chronicles of the times of Solomon, king of Israel. They were buried by a rich Israelite named Eleaser, in the tomb he had built for himself and family, the entrance to which was fifty feet above the water mark of the Nile, and was only found out by an intrepid soldier, who, peering over the rock above, lost his balance, when he caught upon a projection, somewhat larger and about the length of a door knob of modern times. His weight pressed it down, and a cleft appeared in the rock into which when, propped open by his large pistol, he easily passed his body. He immediately struck a light and lit his small wax candle; he saw steps and descended until he came to an outer chamber. As high as he could reach he saw a knob similar to the outer one. He weighed two hundred and four pounds, just sufficient to bring it down. Once more he descended with his light, and below him he saw a wheel; he took hold of it, and moved it round till a small projecting knob was immediately opposite a small indentation a little larger than the button. He pressed it into the indent and two folding doors flew open, and to his astonished view was the tomb of the old Israelite, two daughters and one son, with a vacant tomb for another body, who evidently, after he had fulfilled the wishes of his parent, had by some mischance been kept from burial in his father's tomb. On the breast of the embalmed old man, was a roll of papyrus, and the soldier, who was the youngest son of the Marquis of L., and had enlisted in the romantic Egyptian expedition, was a Greek, Latin and Sanscrit scholar, and was determined the contents of the roll of papyrus should be translated.   He saw jewels of great value, but only brought away a wonderful penholder, of gold, a foot long, with the twelve tribes of Israel elaborately chased and elevated on it; in the top was a sapphire, and inside, when the head was screwed off, were various pens from the quills of a goose.   He, with great care, rolled up the papyrus in his hand-kerchief, and the pen in a piece of linen which he found on a stool near the tomb, and making a rope of the remainder by twisting, he closed the doors after him, and making the linen rope fast to the outside projection, let himself down to the bank of the Nile.   Then, tying his knife on a thick stick, he cut the rope a few feet above his head.   The door, when liberated from his weight, had sprung back to its place.   Reaching the camp, he sought out Bartholomew, a Jew, a fine Hebrew scholar. Binding him to secrecy, and promising him a good reward, after several evenings he elucidated the title page: "Chronicles of the Times of Solomon, the Wise King of Israel, written by myself, Eleazer, son of Samuel."   After the Jew found a good key to the very ancient Hebrew, he translated it as follows, (part of which is completed; and as they have returned to England, the remainder will be transmitted to the writer, who is on terms of great intimacy and friendship with the son of the Marquis of L.):

THE FIRST CHRONICLE OF SOLOMON.

King Solomon, who was a man of wonderful energy and industry, sallied out of his palace with poor vestments on and common sandals, his hair uncombed and disheveled.   It was late at night, for in the day time it was very warm in summer, and dusty in Jerusalem; and especially dusty at that time on account of the immense quantity of material being hauled for the temple he was building.   Having gone a quarter of a mile on the street leading to the Mesopotamia gate, Solomon saw a sandal-maker hard at work, singing even at that late hour.   Solomon went in and inquired the price of making sandals, also as to his prospects in life, and he elicited that by hard labor from day to day, incessantly, that he could earn just enough to live on, and lay by so little that he expected it would be years before he could save enough to marry the maiden he loved, old Levi's daughter. The sandal-maker's name was Benjamin. Solomon inquired where Levi dwelt, and deposited a small piece of folded parchment in a crevice in the wall, with strict injunction to let no one see it except old Levi; and paying him for two pairs of fine finished sandals in advance, Solomon wished the poor man good night and went to the store of old Levi, a shrunken, long-nosed, high-browed, low-statured Israelite, about seventy years of age. He was poring over his accounts for the day, and had many pieces of slate, many tallies, two sticks fitting into each other, full of notches, and rolls of parchment, and some bags of gold he evidently had counted and tallied. Solomon knocked at the door, and the Israelite peered cautiously through the shutters and asked what was wanted. Levi was a dyer. Solomon told him he wanted a hundred sets of fine dyed sandal latchets, and he would pay him the gold for them. Levi rang a small bell, and from an inner apartment Rebecca, the daughter of old Levi, appeared. She knew her father wanted her to watch the new customer and to be a protection to himself; then he unchained the door and let in Solomon; then he chained it again. "What price do you wish to pay?" "I am no haggler," said Solomon, "take my order, make me out a correct account, and receive your gold. Read it over that your daughter may certify that it is correct." The old man read it and looked at Rebecca. She said, "Father, for the gold you can do it so much less." He looked daggers at his child, altered the figures, and said that is very cheap. "To whom shall I send the latchets?" "To Benjamin, the sandal-maker; and look at the parchment stuck in a crevice in his wall. Then you will be pleased to give him your daughter, Rebecca, for his wife." Solomon departed.

The old Israelite next day wanted to take inferior goods to Benjamin but his good daughter, Rebecca, insisted that he should fill the order to the letter; and the old Israelite's curiosity being aroused, he went with his Midian slave and took the sandal trimmings to Benjamin. Old Levi spake unusually kind to him, and seeing the parchment in the crevice, where it had remained unread, he uttered an exclamation of surprise. The large shop and residence next to old Levi's was deeded to Benjamin, and a bag of gold he could get by calling on Copti, the eunuch of the black wife of Solomon the King.

Old Levi became obsequious, and said he would be proud of Benjamin for a son. " You and I had better wait until we prove the deed and get the gold," said Benjamin. " I will hence to a scribe," said old Levi, " and you, Benjamin, go to Copti, the eunuch, at the king's palace." They both went their separate ways, and Copti gave Benjamin the gold and took his acknowledged receipt. And old Levi found by the scribe that the deed was correct and the title clear. So Benjamin located next door to old Levi, and with a hundred trimmings, the best in Jerusalem; a house of his own, and a large bag of gold, he commenced business on an enlarged scale, and in three months he was married to Rebecca, and Solomon, clothed in a neat garb, claimed the privilege of giving the bride away: and he gave her a small purse with a golden S upon it. She was not to open it until three months had passed, and she had proved a good and faithful wife to Benjamin.

At the end of that time poor old Levi was struck with paralysis as he saw the diamonds, rubies, opals and carbuncles the purse contained. The poor old man died and the daughter and Benjamin sold off the old Israelite's property and inherited all his estate, and it was years before they knew that King Solomon had been their benefactor. Thus endeth the first chronicle of Solomon.

SECOND CHRONICLE OF SOLOMON.

On the next night Solomon, dressed in better style—as a middle-class man—took his way to the outskirts of the city by the dim light of the hanging oil lamps at the corner of a narrow intersecting street. Solomon was accosted by a young Israelite of ravishing beauty. Her eye was like the mild gazelle's, yet bright as the evening star: her nose Egyptian, the curve so slight that it added to the beauty of an oval face so perfectly moulded that Astarte could not have had a face more lovely; her teeth regular and white; her brow shone, and shewed intelligence was seated there. She was rather slender, but below the middle height of woman, while jet itself, from Spain, would not shine, when polished, as did her hair. "For Jehovah's sake, for my mother's, and for mine, come to my poor home and abide with me, for my mother is dying of want, and I have nothing to sell but my person to obtain for her a little bread and milk to keep her from death."

Solomon went to her habitation, her mother was reclining on a couch of boards, thin, pale, and attenuated nearly to a shadow. "Here is money," said Solomon, "get bread, wine, and decoction of the bark of the cherry-tree, and bring them quickly." She did, and Solomon assisted her to feed her mother, who revived by the aid of the bread, wine and decoction. "Now, tell me what brought you to this misery?" said Solomon. "When I was sixteen years of age," said Ruth. "I worked for Mordecai, the great vestment-maker, and earned a little regularly, to keep and clothe myself and mother. Young Mordecai took me one evening into an inner room, gave me wine that was drugged, he took away my virtue by committing a rape upon my person, then left and sent a servant to take me home. I went to a doctor of the law and he tried to violate me also. I went to a priest and he nearly succeeded in ravishing me, but I broke from him, bruised and my clothing torn to shreds." "Then why not appeal to the king?" said Solomon. "He is the greatest harlot-monger in the land, and would no doubt have polluted me also. Poverty stings: I sold all my clothing but this garment; all our furniture but those boards that my poor mother sleeps upon." Solomon had twinged but recovered, and said: "Where is your chamber; where is your bed?" She led him to a small offshoot, and on the unpaved floor was a little straw. "So you to-night had no resource but to barter your person for food?" "None," said Ruth; "but now mother has food I will endeavor to obtain something by labor to-morrow." "To-morrow," said Solomon, "go to the postern gate of the palace and ask for Copti; he will give you employment. Now, write down the names of the doctor of the law, of the priest, of young Mordecai, and the residences of them." She did. Solomon left her more gold for their need.

In the morning she saw Copti, and was led into a large hall where young Mordecai, the doctor of law, and the priest were in the hands of the guard. Presently King Solomon came in and Ruth trembled, for it was her friend of the night before, and she remembered what she had said about his being the greatest harlot-monger in the land. He bade her make the statement she did unto the man who befriended her last night. She did until she came to that expression, when she said: "There are some things, most gracious king, will not bear repetition." Solomon admired her candor and her sense. "Let Mordecai marry Ruth, and take her and Ruth's mother to his home, and never let me hear of one unkind word on your part to mother or daughter, and array them both in fine linen," he said to Mordecai.

The doctor of the law and the priest had their heads and beards shaved, and were registered in the army of the king for twenty years without appeal.

In the afternoon Ruth was summoned by Copti, and she found about three hundred of the same age and older, who were workers on vestments for the rich employers in Jerusalem. She also saw her husband, young Mordecai, and his father, and twenty-two rich manufacturers of vestments, on the opposite side of the hall. A few of the laboring girls made statements before Solomon, who was sitting in judgment, with his black Egyptian wife at his left hand. Ruth stated that she had worked three years and had only earned so much. Others that they had labored ten years and were still poor. Then Solomon asked the rich manufacturers for their statements, which Copti had warned them to make on pain of death. Solomon asked them if their records were correct. Then he allowed each to retain ten per cent. as their profit, and the balance was divided among the laborers according to the time they each had labored. When the judgment was ended, Cleo, the black wife of Solomon, called Ruth, and said: "Oh, king! let this young Israelite delight thine eye, and gratify thy amorousness by being concubine. "She is lovely as Venus," said the Egyptian, "I shall enjoy the sight of her in your embrace." The negro woman was straight as an arrow, inclined to flesh, bosom exceedingly developed; her limbs bare (for she wore but one flowing garment), were like those of the Goddess of Morning; her teeth were whiter than ivory; her eyes were melting with love; her lips were like an unstrung bow above a cherry, and the corners of her mouth wore an enduring smile; her face was oval; her nose was straight as a line; her skin smooth as a plum; her arms were plump and dimpled; her finger nails were the perfection of beauty. She was amorous, lecherous, beastly so; and she wished to see her lover, Solomon the King, enjoy the beautiful Israelite. Solomon said: "She is sacred, and I will not violate her home." So Ruth, the beautiful, was dismissed. Thus endeth the second chronicle of Solomon.

THIRD CHRONICLE OF SOLOMON.

Carrying a willow basket, Solomon sought the street where the harlots generally resided. He entered many homes, gave them small sums to tell him their previous history. One Leah was a tall magnificent woman. Sheba's queen was a Scythian beside her. She was from Samaria; a rich vineyard owner had tempted her with wine, and effected her fall by destroying her virginity. After a lapse of a few moons he deserted her for some new victim, and she in shame came to the chief city, Jerusalem. She had been a harlot for three years, and would gladly escape, but knew not how. Solomon saw another, small in stature, black eyes, black hair in masses; she was so voluptuous that she told Solomon she would have variety, it was life to her.

" But it will surely kill," said Solomon.   " I will take a short,
merry life," she answered.   Solomon entered a third house, and
a poor captive from a northern nation sat with her head upon
her hand.   Solomon spake kindly to her and gave her gold, and
she related to him her history.   " I came from the Tin Island*
beyond the pillars of Hercules.   I was playing on the sea-
shore when only fourteen years of age, among the woodbines
which grew wild, gathering violets for a chaplet for my sister's
hair, who dwelt a mile away in the woods, when a boat landed,
and one swift of foot took me prisoner, and in a few minutes I
was aboard their boat.   An arrow from the bow of my sister's
husband cleft the skull of my captor, and in a few minutes we
were away at sea, and I have never seen the white coast of the
Tin Island, and its lovely streams and valleys, from that day to
this.   Four brutes of Tyrians ravished me till we landed
at Tyre.   I escaped and walked to Damascus, but poverty forced
me eventually to Jerusalem, and I shall never see the lovely
home of my childhood again."

Solomon made memorandums of all these persons.   The next
was a girl from near the Sea of Galilee: a strong, robust Israelite; black hair, coarse as a horse's mane: heavy eyebrows: large
lips.   She was going to caress Solomon (much as a bear would
do), when he gave her a piece of gold and left.   She was a perfect animal: lustful from head to foot.

The next house which Solomon visited was one where he
heard an infant prattling in an inner room.   The woman, about
twenty years of age, had painted, as harlots paint: her whiting
covered a dark skin, and it and her paint made her, upon close
scrutiny, look pitiful.   Solomon heard her story.   She was the
daughter of Eleazer, her name was Sarah.   She had been taught
all the Hebrew, Egyptian and Tyrian lore.   She had fine musi-
cal talent, and acquired the name of the Warbler.   At sixteen
she was stately and beautiful: a youth with the form of Apollo,
with eyes like the star of the morning; teeth like flattened
pearls; lips which seemed only suitable for kissing: a voice mu-
sical as the nightingales.   " *He* was false, and in two years he
seduced me.   Then when his lust was gratified, and I was near

* England.

to become a mother, he left me." Solomon pitied this woman much, and gave her gold enough to leave her calling, and furnish a small habitation for herself and child.

At the next house Solomon heard an uproar, and going in perceived three young females wringing their hands: there were three of them, for the fourth had just hung herself. Solomon took the knife from his girdle, severed the silken cord, sent for restoratives, and saw the almost a child resuscitated; then he heard their history: each had been vain and seduced: the youngest (twelve years of age) only a month ago, by young Jacob, and he had married another. Solomon left, and the next day had every harlot in the city brought to the great hall. Then he ordered those who wished to leave the life they led to go to the right. Amongst them were the four young girls: the young mother appeared not, as she had left her harlotry; the girl from the White or Tin Islands, and the magnificent woman from Samaria, and a hundred more: while several hundred who loved their harlotry and shame-facedness, remained on the left. Then Solomon provided means for all who wished to leave their sinful life. With a recommendation from Copti, he forced the vintner of Samaria to marry the one he had seduced: the girl from the Tin Islands he sent home in a Syrian ship with an officer of his household to protect her until she landed. She prayed all her life for Solomon, her redeemer: he asked as a favor from the king of Tyre, for the four men who had ravished her: he emasculated them, and then for seven years, with a brand upon their foreheads, he had them work on the highways. Then Solomon issued an edict that no harlot should reside or walk within one mile of the Temple, and owners should be imprisoned who rented any house or room to harlots, and pay a hundred pieces of gold into the king's treasury: and the watchmen of the city and officers of the law who saw any person from twelve years of age and upwards who visited such harlots' homes should take both him and the harlot, and they should be fined and imprisoned; and if it were proved by Copti that any watchman or officer of the law evaded the edict, they should be imprisoned, fined and dismissed from their offices.

All harlots should be registered and examined as to their health by two physicians; one aged, one younger, and in a manner the least offensive. The young Israelites and aged debauchees who frequently support such places, should, when caught, be registered in the Band of Lechery, and copies should be hung up outside of the great hall of justice. Thus would Jerusalem become more free from lust, and the occupation of harlotry unprofitable. Thus endeth the third chronicle of Solomon.

FOURTH CHRONICLE OF SOLOMON.

Solomon, dressed as an artizan, went out earlier than usual, and visited many homes, and one grand lament met his ear. They wondered why the king allowed those of princely wealth to buy up all the olives, all the dates, all the corn from Egypt, the honey and manna from Midian, and the cattle from Dan to Beersheba, and from Lebanon to the territory of the Coshites; and Solomon was grieved. He saw that the princes in wealth in Israel combined and bought up all things in general use among the people, and sold at an excessive profit, which being resold by small dealers, cost enormous prices, and the wailing was just and it pervaded the whole of the land. And Solomon changed his raiment and sought out the grandees that fattened and feasted on the blood of Israel, and broke down the spirit of the people. He inquired into their profits and they felt offended, saying it was not any one's matter but their own, and that a tithe would cover all their profits on olives, dates, corn, honey and on cattle. Then Solomon sent out messengers on fleet horses and gathered information from all the cities and villages in the kingdom, and he found the complaint was universal. Then Solomon called all the grandees to the hall and they saw that the king was the inquirer, and they trembled. Then Solomon bade them bring a correct account of all the olives, dates, corn, honey and cattle they had purchased, and the price they paid for each quality. So he found out all there was in the land, and he ordered ten per cent., or a tithe, to be allowed as their profit, and it was sold to the people throughout the land, and no persons were allowed to purchase any of these necessaries for speculation only sufficient to resell in their own localities; and the hearts of the people were glad, but the nobles or rich men waxed wroth and plotted to kill Solomon; but the ring-leaders were captured and put to death, and during Solomon's reign they never added more than a tithe on their purchases. Thus endeth the fourth chronicle of Solomon.

FIFTH CHRONICLE OF SOLOMON.

Many complaints had been made to Copti respecting the difficulty in convicting those guilty of theft, of rape, of sodomy and murder, in consequence of the young doctors of the law so harrassing witnesses that they in their fright sometimes contradicted in minor points their own evidence; and how many upright men had been wrongfully imprisoned, and had their characters so blackened by the declarations of these same loose-tongued youths, that innocent men were almost afraid they must be guilty. Solomon thereupon determined to attend the same courts and judge for himself, and so he put on the dress of a chief doctor of the law and entered a court. The case was a young low-browed Israelite, who had stolen a purse. The owner testified as to the amount and number of pieces, but the only person who saw him take the purse was a young girl of fifteen, young and maidenly. The young lawyer said:

"Sarah, do you know the prisoner?"

"No."

"Then, what are you here to testify to?"

"I saw him take the purse."

"Is this the purse?"

"Yes."

"Will you swear this is the purse?"

"I feel certain. It is the color and size."

" Can you tell that purse from this?" (producing one about the same size.)

" No."

" Then you don't know which purse it was of these two that was stolen?"

" No."

" Where were you when, as you pretend, you saw the prisoner take the purse?"

" In my chamber. It overlooks Samuel's room, and he had left it a moment, when the prisoner rushed in and stole the purse from the stool on which it was lying."

" How old was the person who stole the purse?"

" About the age of this youth."

" Don't you think he was older?"

" No."

" Did he have the same vestments on?"

" No. He wore a tunic of brown."

" Can you positively swear this is the youth?"

" I think he is."

" But you must not think. You must be positive. You are not quite sure that this youth you want to drive to prison is the one who stole Samuel's purse?"

" I think he is."

" But you are not going to swear him to prison?"

" No."

" That will do. You evidently don't know anything about it."

Solomon took the judgment seat. All were amazed.

" Who is that fellow who took the judgment seat?" asked Benjamin, the young law doctor, loud enough for Solomon to hear.

An old doctor wished to see Solomon's credentials, and then bowed low.

" Arrest Benjamin for contempt."

Solomon was obeyed. " Let him stand by the prisoner."

" Jacob, are you guilty?"

" No."

" Maiden, come near. What is your name?"

" Sarah."

" Where were you when you saw the prisoner take the purse ? "

" In my chamber."

" Do you feel certain that the prisoner is the person who took the purse from the stool where Samuel had left it? "

" Yes. I cannot be mistaken. I saw him clearly, and I have seen him pass by Samuel's door many times."

" That will do. Samuel, how came you to leave the purse upon the stool? "

" I wanted to replenish my fire, and lest I might drop my purse as I was going, I left it for a moment on the stool. I returned in time to see Jacob turn onto the next street. I followed with a minister of the law, and in an hour he was a prisoner, and I found a piece of my gold where he had paid it out."

" How know you it was your piece? "

" I accidentally dropped it in the embers of the fire yesterday, and before I could take it out the heat had discolored the edge of it."

" Let Jacob be punished with stripes, and Benjamin be stripped of his robe, and go back to his teacher for seven years, to learn that the truth by the simplest means and evidence is what is needed to convict or set free one that is accused; and it is unwise and unjust to terrify or harrass a witness to that extent it oftimes tends to counteract the evidence, and set free on society the vilest of criminals." ·

So Solomon had all the doctors of the law assembled in the large hall, and four prisoners brought in to be tried—a murderer, a robber, one who had violated a maiden, and one who had abused his neighbor. He allowed each doctor to plead for the accused ten minutes. Then for the accuser ten minutes, and so on, limiting each case to an hour. Some of the lawyers were fair in their questioning, and did not take undue advantage of the simplicity of a witness; others would try to intimidate, to puzzle, to bewilder, and make their evidence not tally; others, in vehemence and declamation went on soaring, and actually said nothing in their time allotted; others were so crafty.

that they tried to ensnare witnesses and make black appear
white; a few had the uprightness to question fairly, and speak
kindly, making endeavors to elicit the truth. These were re-
tained as advisors, but all the rest which Solomon had noted for
four long hours, he sent back to learn to be honest in their questioning, and not to practice law again for seven years. During
that time just verdicts were given; none were afraid to give correct evidence, as they did not fear abuse. Thus endeth the
fifth chronicle of Solomon.

SIXTH CHRONICLE OF SOLOMON.

Complaints came to the king of those who manufactured
chariots, utensils, and all the necessary articles for a household, especially in articles of iron and tin and steel, and of those
of the potter, and it was found by men of sagacity and wisdom
that a duty had been laid by the officials of the land upon the
swords and wares of Damascus; on tools used by carpenters
from Tyre, and even the cedar from Lebanon; upon the cordage
for nets; upon parchment for writing; upon jewels of silver and
gold; upon their lamps and candlesticks; nearly all were brought
from Tyre or Petra, and the burden of paying two amounts to the
few who fabricated articles of necessity, on account of the duty;
which, but for the duty, could come so much cheaper from Tyre,
from Damascus, from Petra, and from Egypt. So Solomon had
those who fabricated chariots and wains, pruners and swords,
shears and bucklers, implements of husbandry and family utensils, brought from all parts of his kingdom, to state why they
wished the duties to remain on what they fabricated, when
their admission free would benefit so much the people of Israel.
They pulled long faces, and said they could barely live, and
that should the duties be taken off the country would be filled
with everything at so low a price that they would be ruined.
So Solomon sent them back to bring a record within one moon
of all their manufactures, of their goods on hand, what means

they had when they commenced to manufacture goods; what houses and lands; what gold and silver they had, and all they possessed. He found there were less than six hundred fabricators of steel, of iron, of leather, and potteries, on a large scale; that there were over two million of Israelites who used these articles, and many were exchanged with Midianites, with Philistria, with Petra, Mesopotamia and Arabia. Solomon found that most of these rich fabricators had little to commence with; that most of them were rich, many very rich; and Solomon had them divide amongst their workers all their surplus wealth over a tithe on their money in use, each year. The duties were taken off, and the country was soon full of all those things which were in use by the people, and the products of Israel were given in exchange, so that the tax on revenue soon filled the coffers of Solomon; the mass of the people were happy; general prosperity prevailed, and the country was full of gold and silver. Thus endeth the sixth chronicle of Solomon.

SEVENTH CHRONICLE OF SOLOMON.

It came to the ears of the king that a great number of his people had become wine-bibbers, and that wine was sold in any quantity to suit the means of the purchaser; that much of it was adulterated; that the youths of Israel, like Noah of old, were often in a state of drunkenness, and did incest, sodomy, murder, rape, bearing false witness against their neighbors, perjury, theft, and that they dishonored their parents and worshiped strange gods; and the heart of Solomon was sad. So he rambled among the dealers and saw aged men, with one foot in the grave, gulping down the deleterious mixtures called wine, and men who labored hard for a trifling pittance spent most of their earnings in the vile trash vended unto them, while their children were barefooted and without sandals, or scarcely any vestments to cover their nakedness, and their profanity mingled with their ignorant boasts; and Solomon saw little children try to lead their drunken parents to their miserable abodes; and the king saw the sons of the grandees, rich owners and vendors of goods, all in a state of mawkishness and blaspheming Jehovah as often as they opened their mouths, and they were mixed up with the skum of Jerusalem; and it grieved the heart of Solomon sorely, for he could not see clearly how to remedy so great and so growing an evil. So he had every dealer in and vendor of wine brought to the great hall to explain their circumstances from the time they first vended the drinks to that day, and he stripped them of their ill-gotten wealth and sent them to scrub the decks of his vessels for three years with no pay but their food. Then he had licenses for new vendors of wine at one hundred pieces of gold; all those who adulterated wine were to be imprisoned and forfeit all their stock and worldly goods, and to be sent as hewers of wood for three years in the forests of Lebanon; and every one, old and young, who drank and became drunk, their names should be placed in the lists of drunkards, and exposed on all the corners of the city, and be made servitors in his armies for three years. Thus was pure wine only sold; vendors were few; and drunkards were reformed by becoming industrious. Thus endeth the seventh chronicle of Solomon.

EIGHTH CHRONICLE OF SOLOMON.

And lo, and behold! there was wailing in the land on account of the great usury extorted from the people; they giving their goods, their furniture, their jewels and their utensils for security for small amounts of money loaned them. And Solomon obtained a list from Copti of a hundred who had borne extortions year after year, until they were plunged in misery, so that many took their own lives, not being able to endure the anguish and misery they had; and they were brought into the great hall, and their memorandums were displayed, and he saw that all their furniture, their goods, their chattles, their implements, their gold and their silver ornaments and precious stones, even their houses, were in the hands of the usurers; and Solomon had their wives and children and their dependents brought in, and their squalor and abjectness distressed the king, and he ordered them to be fed and placed on the right hand of the hall. And Solomon gathered together every one who loaned, even every usurer in Jerusalem was brought in and placed on the left hand of the hall. Their garments were rich, their bellies were prominent, and their cheeks were rounded with fat; and Solomon ordered every one to show what he had when he became a usurer, and what he was worth that day; and Solomon found that the poor had become poorer, that the rich had become richer daily, and that some of the poor had paid many times over in usury what their goods were pledged for originally. And Solomon ordered the usurers to give back all the goods they held, and to every one all that each had charged over a half tithe for a year, and to come the next day to the hall, in their plainest garments; and the poor were comforted, and received their beds and their furniture, their implements and their ornaments; and all they had paid over half a tithe per annum as usury; and the next day the usurers and money-lenders appeared in plain apparel, and the king ordered them to be stripped and prison apparel, with stripes, put upon them, and to be branded with "usurer" on each man's brow, and to break stones on the streets of Jerusalem for three years, with a ball and chain upon their legs, as though they were the most debased and guilty sinners in Jerusalem; and Solomon ordered a fund to be set apart to be loaned in small sums to the really necessitous, without usury; and Solomon made an edict that nothing in Jerusalem should be purchased on credit, but paid for at the time of the purchase, and that thereafter no debt should be collectible; that all houses and lands thus bought should be recorded, and after this no one could own any land or houses unless recorded as paid for in money; nor any one, either Israelite or Gentile, should be held as a slave from that day during the whole of his reign. Thus endeth the seventh chronicle of Solomon.

EIGHTH CHRONICLE OF SOLOMON.

Complaints had been made to Copti about the weights and measures throughout the whole of Jerusalem. So Solomon, dressed as a countryman, took a basket and went to eminent dealers, who, full of suavity, seemed the essence of innocence. Solomon had one weight and bought that amount, and when he doubted the justness of the weights of the dealers they became irritated and abusive; but Solomon fearing not weighed with his own weight, and insisted upon having the full quantity for the price they sold at. Most of them were light, and yet when they bought they had weights heavier than the true ones; so satisfying himself of the general dishonesty of the vendors, he had every one's name brought to him who vended in Jerusalem; then sent his guards and had every one brought before him, and all their weights and measures, and having placed one of the just judges on the bench, Solomon, dressed as a countryman, pointed out those who had tried to wrong him; but they still thinking him a rustic, swore to the accuracy of their weights, and pleaded that an unknown countryman's word should not be taken before theirs who were old inhabitants, and whose reputation was unsullied. Then Solomon passed into another room and came out again appareled as the king, and the high dignitary gave up his seat to the king. Then the false dealers of whom Solomon had bought besought him to pardon their unseemly language, but he answered them not, and of six hundred dealers in Jerusalem only forty-two had weights and measures correct. So the king made them give a written order to Copti for all their provisions to be brought to the great square at the rear of his palace, and Solomon divided all their ill-gotten gains amongst the poor of Jerusalem, according to the number dependent upon them. The forty-two just dealers were rewarded by Solomon. Upon the brow of the others he had branded "false weight and measure." They were sent with their beards and heads shaved and prison clothing put on to go on a cruise as laborers for three years without pay; and Solomon cured their unjust ways during the whole of his reign. Thus endeth the eighth chronicle of Solomon.

NINTH CHRONICLE OF SOLOMON.

Whereas it came to the ears of the king that the scribes and expounders of the law eat up the fat of the land, and became rich, and they were as locusts in the land; that they bred dissension and strife, and suborned false witnesses, and laid traps for the guileless and unwary, and endeavored to get gold from innocent men and women under threats of misstatements respecting their dealings, their faith, and their chastity; and people dreading their abilities to falsify and their forensic eloquence, and their lack of truth, submitted to be plundered by these ravenous sharks, who would plead for a murderer, knowing that he was a murderer; who would plead for a robber, knowing him to be a thief; who would plead for men who perjured themselves, who moved their neighbor's landmarks; for those they knew were guilty of adultery; and would plead for those who broke every one of the commandments; and would endeavor by their skill in language and by their bland manners to impose upon the judges; many of whom by their simplicity were easily imposed upon, and oftimes unjust judgments were given. So Solomon had the whole of the scribes and expounders of the law examined by judges who were old, upright and learned in the law. Solomon had them examined one by one, and most of them were set aside, as neither having capacity, judgment, or moral honesty; and Solomon adjudged them to be disrobed, and for seven years they should be menders of the public roads, and at the end of that period they should enter into some honest avocation, and never again enter that of a scribe or expounder of the law. Thus during the remainder of Solomon's reign justice in the simplest manner was administered, and if any were dissatisfied with the judgment, Solomon made an edict that five men, if a man; five women, if a woman, should hear and pronounce by three majority, and the judge should sentence or liberate from their verdict. Thus endeth the ninth chronicle of Solomon.

TENTH CHRONICLE OF SOLOMON.

Solomon felt glad in his heart. Jerusalem and Judea, from Dan to Beersheba, from Tadmor and the Red Sea unto the borders of Tyre, were prosperous, and the people of Israel were comparatively happy, when Copti learned that there was great dissatisfaction with husbands and fathers and young men on account of the amorousness of the Levites for their wives and their daughters, and their betrothed ones were seduced in the dwellings appertaining to the synagogues, and the evil had become a crying one, and children were born to the rabbis by unmarried women, and by the daughters of Israel; and as Solomon was a great debauchee, a whoremonger, and had a great number of concubines, from the grandest and from the petite, from the blue-eyed of the North and from the piercing black-eyed ones of the South; from Chaldea and from Mesopotamia; from Persia and from Egypt; from Petra and Arabia, and even from the Scythians and from the Greek Islands: many came to see the grandeur and magnificence of his palaces, which were builded with ivory from Abyssinia, with gold from Sheba; of gems from the eastern lands (where the geni dwelt), and amber from the seas beyond the pillars of Hercules. The beautiful woodwork, with its elaborate carvings, was from Sidon. The jewels he and his wives and his concubines wore were fashioned in Egypt, and the fine linen also. The fruits of all islands were brought him in vessels from Tyre; spices, myrrh and frankincense and spikenard from Arabia, and fruits from the isles of the sea; and in the Songs of Solomon is described the love of the black Egyptian for him. So Solomon brought every priest and rabbi and Levite to Jerusalem, and he commanded on pain of death, and it was proclaimed by Copti, that every married woman, and every virgin who had been seduced and debauched by the priests, the rabbis and the Levites, should state the same in the great hall : and seven hundred and eighty wives and virgins who had been debauched and seduced by these soft-tongued priests, under pretense of religious duty, out of pity, others because the language of the rabbis had been 'amorous and lecherous, and in the outhouses of the synagogues, and even in the temples, when awe came over them, and opportunity offered, at the houses of their husbands when away, and at the schools in after-hours where the young and innocent virgins were beguiled and their offspring were brought forth untimely and abortive, while others were strangled, and thrown from the rocks ; some were buried in the gardens in the rear of the houses of the priests, and the mass of the women and the maidens were polluted, as thousands had been before ; for the learning of the priests made them soft tongued, and as expounders of the Law and as teachers they had admission to the most private chambers of their victims ; and when persuasion availed not, they by noxious herbs would scatter the senses of their victims ; then they debauched the wives or the widows and destroyed the virginity of the maidens. And Solomon assuming that although his palace was filled with harlots, yet as the king could do no wrong according to the idea of the time, he went on with his own seductions and debauchery, and he ordered the priests and the rabbis and the Levites who were guilty of seduction and violating virgins, to be made eunuchs, and for those who had betrayed wives and widows, that for seven years they should sweep the streets of Jerusalem, and cart off the rubbish through the gates, and be branded on their brows with the word " Lechery." Thus through the remainder of King Solomon's reign were maidens and widows and wives, as a general thing, free from pollution. Yet even with the stringent laws against them would many young priests brave the edicts and seduce virgins and debauch wives, although when found out they would be made to sweep the streets or be branded as others had been, for such is the force of amorousness, that for an hour of guilty pleasure they would have to endure years of misery. So Solomon had every wife or widow, and all who had not lost their virginity with the priests but had been harlots unto them, to be branded with the word "harlot" on their foreheads ; and as many could not bear the shame they took their own lives ; others could not live with their husbands, so they became harlots in very deed. Solomon also made an edict that the priest should, after his term of degradation had passed, if alive and unmarried, marry one of the women he had seduced.

Thus endeth the Tenth Chronicle of Solomon.

THE ELEVENTH CHRONICLE OF SOLOMON.

And it came to the ears of Copti that great numbers of un-
skilled men, under pretense of being physicians, were actually
killing off the people of Israel, and that they were in collusion
with those who sold noxious herbs, or salts or other professed
articles, to cure ; and with witches who pretended to. know
remedies for every ailment : and that they were also guilty of
unburying the dead, and of cutting up the bodies of those
buried, to gain a knowledge of the healing art. And Solomon
found out from Copti who were sick, and after the physicians
had been called, he listened to their statements, and took notes
of the same, and then called skilled physicians and had them
investigate. And Solomon found that in many cases the young
aspirants to the healing art were trying experiments, and others
were doing what was detrimental : and so Solomon commanded
the youthful doctors to swallow their own medicines, and in
many cases they became sick unto death. So Solomon gathered
together all the practitioners of Jerusalem and the other large
cities of Judea, and from the learned physicians he had certain
questions propounded to them ; and the answers were written
and sealed, with the name of each healer upon it, and those who
had answered according to the then well-established rules of
physic were allowed to practice, but the rest were branded with
the word "quack" upon their brows, and were dismissed from
the healing art forever. And it was found throughout the land
that the average of human life, when the people were numbered
in two decades, was longer, and the people more numerous than
when being slaughtered by incompetent physicians.

Thus endeth the Eleventh Chronicle of Solomon.

THE TWELFTH CHRONICLE OF SOLOMON.

And it came to pass, as there was peace in Israel, and extor-
tioners, and those who were dishonest in weight or measure, de-
frauders in wine and usurers, debauchees of the scribes, and
witless practitioners of the law and physic, were punished, that
the people became rich, and men who had been abroad brought

back the manners and habits of those amongst whom they had dwelt, and they brought into Israel games of chance, and in time those who had become expert established themselves in all the cities of Israel, and with bits of wood that were numbered the expert who followed the business had six chances to the one chance of the untutored. Still they would wager and lose, then wager again. Poor men would lose the earnings of a week on a single throw; and the hearts of the gamesters became hardened, and when they had won all a poor man's earnings, all a rich man's wealth, many would take their own lives so unhappy they were at being stripped of their gold, their silver, their gems, their furniture and their bedding, their houses and their lands, their vineyards, their cattle, and even the chastity of their wives, which they would chance on the number of spots on a bit of wood. And the gamester would chuckle and rake in all the gold, and silver, and gems into their bags underneath the tables, where the bits of wood were spun round; then they would wager against deeds of houses and lands, and many who were once rich became poor, and some in revenge would slay the expert, and many take away their own lives. So Solomon went as a laborer to a House of Chance, and when he had lost what a laborer would lose, he pleaded to the owner of the gambling place for as much as would buy him a loaf of bread and a few dates; but the gambler told him if he had no more to wager to begone, for they had room only for players. Then Solomon changed his garments and went to the gambling places of the rich, and lost in proportion, and he pleaded for a portion as it was the birthday of his daughter and he had forgotten to put by enough to buy a present for her: but they heeded him not for their hearts were harder than adamant. And Solomon found the chances were many against the wagerer. Sometimes the gamblers would spin and Solomon saw that they used a different piece from those the public wagered with; and Solomon lifted one of their pieces and found the side they wagered on was weighted, and Solomon said they were not honest. When the gamblers threatened Solomon, he blew a whistle and Copti came in with fifty guards, and Solomon said take these men and put them to death. And Copti detailed twenty men who took them to the house of penalty, and they were put to death. Copti crept near to Solomon, for he knew what desperate villains the gamblers were ; and when Solomon had proved that not one gambler had one trait of goodness or honesty in him, he had them all brought to the great hall, and all their furniture and their gambling pieces, and all their gold and their silver and gems, and deeds of houses and lands, and had all those who had wagered and lost brought in, and he gave back to every one what he had wagered and lost, and he had every man who had wagered given many stripes, and told them if they were caught gambling again he would set them to break stones upon the roads for a year.　But every gambler Solomon had branded upon his brow with the word "gambler," and sent every one, with heavy chains about his legs, to break stones for ten years, with an edict that if they ever entered that occupation again they should be put to death.

Thus endeth the Twelfth Chronicle of Solomon.

THIRTEENTH CHRONICLE OF SOLOMON.

And lo and behold! as the good laws of Solomon added to the wealth and happiness of Israel, and they forgot their simplicity and branched out into all kinds of extravagance in food, in their furniture, their ornaments, and especially in dress, and although the men became somewhat fantastical, yet it was the extreme riches and fashion of the women that caused eventually so much misery ; for they would puff out their vestments behind until they looked awfully deformed, their bosoms were stuffed with floss, even their waists and their backs and shoulders ; and no man could tell the shape of any woman until he married her and her superabundance was taken off ; their teeth were replaced by imitations, and they practiced before mirrors of polished brass to open their mouths wide in conversation, until they showed their false teeth incessantly.　They also carmined their faces to make them have a rosy hue, and the white dust from the Tin Islands ground to powder for their arms, their legs and their bosoms and faces, to make them look fair ;

but it gave them the appearance of harlots, and by the whore-
mongers they were ofttimes mistaken for harlots, and were insulted and abused and followed to the very doors of their husbands and father. They also had knobs placed in the centre of
their shoe soles and they would tilt forward and often fall, instead of having the sole of their shoes flat like the human foot ;
and many lost their health by painting, and their complexions
were untimely injured by the use of cosmetics ; and instead of
being thought prettier they were loathed by the male sex for
their wickedness, and spoken of contemptuously for want of
sense, and none were loved or respected with sincerity so much
as those who dressed with neatness and wore vestments which
displayed their natural shape ; those who were rich bought the
most costly clothing that could be purchased in Tyre or Sidon,
or in Egypt, and they bought the hair from dead females and
dead animals and had it made into curls and masses, as near the
color of their own hair as could be ; but it always looked dead
and unnatural, and the exact shade could never be matched, so
that every one who wore dead hair could be detected. Many
caught loathsome diseases, even leprosy and itch, from wearing
the hair of dead people. The tradesmen or vendors' wives aped
the manners and dress of the very rich, and ruined their husbands by their extravagance. Many for dress and jewels would
barter their honor and break the hearts of their husbands, and
many took their own lives, and some slew the seducers of their
wives ; and many young maidens were enticed by dress, by gold,
and by jewels to give up their virginity, and eventually, though
well versed in the lore of the Israelites, and of the Egyptians,
of Tyre, of Sidon, and of Damascus, and of the Cushites of
Arabia, they would become harlots in early life, and die early of
disease ; and their head gear they would raise higher and higher
until it became a pinnacle. And the servitors and vendors'
wives imitated the richest, and those from Egypt, Palmyra and
Petra, and they had to bend their bodies to go under their door-
ways. But vanity, vanity was the lot of woman from Eve until
now ; and Solomon found with all his wisdom that it was an evil
of such magnitude that he scarcely knew how to control it.
Then he had all those who had the costliest garments brought

to the great hall, and their husbands on the left, and Solomon requested each one to state what his income was; and all those wives who had vestments and jewels beyond a certain portion of it, he had them stripped of their vestments and jewels, and arrayed them in sackcloth for a year, on the back of which he had branded, " Pride brought on this fall."

Then he took a second grade, and all who had brought their husbands down, and some to poverty, he had wear sackcloth for a year and branded "folly and pride." The projections on garments became less and the feathers of the ostrich disappeared; the carmine gave way to nature's color, and the dead hair was thrown to the dogs, and the Israelitish women became beautiful and shapely, and seductions were less, and the vendors and architects flourished, and husbands had peace at home.

Thus endeth the Thirteenth Chronicle of Solomon.

FOURTEENTH CHRONICLE OF SOLOMON.

In Jerusalem and the large cities where the pavements and roads and sewers had to be made, the officials who managed the affairs of a city or a town or a village, made contracts with road-makers, and builders, and sewer-builders, for lumber, for bricks, for stone, and for hollow tubes; and they plundered the cities and towns by agreeing with the contractors for much more than the real cost; and they made hundreds of pieces of gold, and many pounds of silver, which they received as bribes for contracts. Then they made false entries to delude and rob those who paid their tithes to their robber rulers; and it had gone on from year to year, until they waxed bolder and bolder, until the city managers and head men and contractors stunk in the nostrils of the people. And Solomon had all the contractors of public works and all the city, town, and village fathers brought to the great hall; and they had to produce their accounts for his whole reign. And Solomon found the people of Israel had been cheated and plundered until the contractors and officials had become exceedingly rich; then he ordered all their ill-gotten wealth to be given back to the people, and he had the

contractors and officials beaten with many stripes and branded
with the word "swindlers," on their brows, and forced them to
make and mend roads, make bridges and sewers, and to do all
such work for the nation in their vicinity of a public nature,
for seven years, at the price of labor and materials, the contractors and officials receiving only laborers' wages for that
period, and every workman should be paid on Friday, or the
sixth day, at sundown, and rest all day on Saturday or the seventh day.

Thus endeth the Fourteenth Chronicle of Solomon.

FIFTEENTH CHRONICLE OF SOLOMON.

On account of the growing wealth in Israel and the surrounding territory, under the dominion of Solomon, the people
of every class in the land desired to travel to Tyre and Sidon,
Palmyra, Damascus, Petra, and throughout Egypt; and by
means of relays of horses, and wains and chariots the people
were passed from the Mediterranean to Mesopotamia, from the
limits of Tyre to Upper Egypt. And those who had wealth
bought up the conveyances, the horses, the mules, the asses
and camels, from Dan to Beersheba. Others had cross lines
from the sea to the great roads leading to Nineveh and
Babylon, and their gold accumulating, they bought up the com-
munications one after another, until three or four rich men became owners of all the roads. Then they became so extremely
opulent that they had power to influence almost all the officials
throughout Israel. So King Solomon, who wondered at their
immense fortunes, as they had builded themselves palaces of
marble, and had pillars of polished granite from Egypt, their
chairs and their lounges and bedsteads were of carved ivory and
inlaid with gold and silver and with costly pearl, their chairs
of pure gold, so massive that they could not carry them with
convenience, and the diamonds in their rings were extremely
valuable: their other rings were set with rubies and opals, with
sapphires, onyx, and with carbuncles, and their value was very
great: their mirrors of polished brass reflected the beauty of

their wives and their concubines and their costly furniture; their
scrips were in frames of ivory and pearl and inlaid with gems ;
their earrings were beautiful amethysts, their armlets were massive gold set with jewels, and their anklets blazed with diamonds:
even the soles of their shoes were inlaid at the sides with gold
and gems ; their drinking cups were of massive gold, and their
trenchers and dishes of gold and silver, their knives of the steel
of Damascus, and the handles were solid chased gold, the history of Israel from the time of Laban and Lot to the taking
possession of Canaan, was carved and raised in gold on the
handles ; their shades from the sun were of silk from the rising
sun land, and the handles of ivory and gold, with a large dia-
mond in the end ; their fans were made in Etruria, where the
setting sun casts its golden light over the tops of the fiery
mountains ; and amber from the seas beyond the pillars of Hercules was inserted in all their utensils ; choice plants from the
east of Arabia, and aromatic plants from Arabia itself : every
one of their houses were palaces, and the aroma of sweet-scented
herbs and lovely roses from Sharon and Damascus made their
gardens miniature paradises.   Yet they were not happy, but
were grasping forever for more gold ; and they became haughty
and insolent, and treated all men with scorn.   So Solomon, in
a plain vestment, called on the wealthiest, whose name was
Ezekiel, and Solomon said he came for a catalogue of his houses,
his lands, of his jewels, and of his gold and silver, of his furniture, and of all he possessed, for the king wished to obtain a
knowledge of who was the richest man in his kingdom.   But
Ezekiel treated him rudely, and said, surely King Solomon, if
he wished to communicate with him, would have sent a grandee
and not a simple vendor, as his appearance showed him to be.
But Solomon insisted upon taking the catalogue with him, and
was willing to wait until the sands of the hourglass had passed
through twice; but Ezekiel was wroth and bade Solomon begone.
So when Ezekiel had retired to his couch amid his rose spray
fountains and his embroidered linen, on a bed of down, and the
carvings of his furniture so delicate that it was termed wood
work tracery, and was of rosewood, of ebony, of sandalwood, of
the cedar of Lebanon, and of the knobs of the cherry tree; an

alarm was sounded and his door was broken in by the soldiers of King Solomon, a dress was provided by Copti of the coarsest sackcloth, and all his books, his tallies, his parchments, his gold, and his silver, and his gems, were taken to the great hall: his wife and his children were allowed to inhabit a small, neat outhouse, with beds and furniture for comfort, but the servants and slaves and concubines were dismissed with a piece of gold each, and they went to other friends or relatives in Jerusalem; and the king's seal was placed upon the palace of Ezekiel and he was taken to the great hall and kept there for judgment. And the other owners of roads who had millions in gold were also brought to the great hall in their own vestments, as they had not insulted the king; but their palaces were sealed with the king's seal, and their slaves, and their servants and their concubines were given each a piece of gold and liberated. Then Solomon, for his government, took possession of every road, and those who labored were paid the worth of their labor, and Solomon added to the carrying of persons the carriage of articles of trade and of messages from one city to another, and from friends to friends: so that any sealed message could be sent from Damascus to the Upper Nile, and from the sea to the Mesopotamia gate, for a small piece of silver. And Solomon had all the gold, and silver, and jewels, and furniture, and houses and lands belonging to these opulent men sold and their palaces also, and all over a sufficiency to start them in a small business as a vendor, except Ezekiel, was divided amongst those who had done all the work for Ezekiel and the other rich road owners; but Ezekiel had to work as cook in the scullery of the palace for seven years, and his earnings were delivered to his wife at the end of every moon. After awhile any who had shown good behavior for a year, as vendors, except Ezekiel, were employed on the roads they used to own, by the king; and at the end of seven years, as Ezekiel had been industrious and prudent, Solomon forgave him, and he became a worker for the government also.

Thus were the great monopolies overthrown and the government of Solomon enriched, and the people were carried, and their missives and goods, for much less cost, and safer than before.

Thus endeth the Fifteenth Chronicle of Solomon.

SIXTEENTH CHRONICLE OF SOLOMON.

And Solomon rejoiced greatly in the changes he had made
in Israel, and he drove through Jerusalem with his queens, and
his ebony wife, and the people rejoiced in the great changes he
had made in Israel, and the king passed to some great town and
returned until he had made the circuit of his kingdom; and he
would have been regaled in princely style, but Solomon sent
Copti in advance and instructed those with whom Solomon
would tarry not to spend their substance in producing rich food
or buying adornments so as to use their silver or their gold un-
necessarily, but in a neat and loving manner to entertain him
and his household.   And Solomon always left some present of
more value than his entertainment; but he found that the
youths and the maidens were but illy instructed; so Solomon
sent to Babylon, to Tyre, and Sidon, to Nineveh, Damascus, to
Petra and the great cities of Egypt, and to the seaports in
Spain for manuscripts, and he had them copied by the priests
and the Levites on parchment; and he also arranged it so that
every child between ten and fourteen, should go to the halls of
learning, and should not be employed in any of the workshops
until that age.   And in addition to the knowledge of Hebrew
they should read the laws of Moses, and the history of Israel,
the histories of Egypt, and of Syria, and Philistria, of Tyre, of
Sidon, of Edom, of Petra, of Babylon, and Nineveh, and of the
Cushites of Arabia, travels to distant lands, to Arabia and
Europe, as far as the pillars of Hercules, also even to Persia and
the Scythians of the North, and to the land of ivory and gold;
and they were instructed in seafaring, in the art of healing, the
study of herbs, of animals, and the study of the law, so that
they could read to the people; also, in the rudiments of art, in
the cutting of wood and stone, in pottery and in working of
steel, and iron, and brass; in leather, and in tanning, and in
working in gold and silver; so that when the Israelites traveled
in after life among surrounding nations they might excel in history, in a knowledge of Hebrew, in conversation; and the Songs
of Solomon, and the Psalms of his father David were to be
committed to memory, so that the Israelites might be considered

wise wherever they traveled. And he ordered that none should travel unless they had sufficient means, so that none of the Israelites should be looked upon as beggars. And the fame of King Solomon spread far and near, and all the young children and youth were well instructed.

And Solomon had heard of far-off lands away to the East: so he gathered together great philosophers and many learned men, and he had strong ships built by the Tyrians on the Red Sea, and he sent warlike men to guard the learned, and his ships were manned by the mariners of Tyre and Sidon, and much food and gold and silver was sent in his ships, and they arrived in a thickly inhabited country which had old temples cut in the rocks, for worship, of which no man could tell; and where precious stones were almost playthings for children. So the gold of Solomon purchased a mass of precious stones, that when they reached Israel, and Egypt, and Tyre, were increased in value a thousand fold. So Solomon determined to build habitations for the artisans of Jerusalem on little mounts and in valleys, and to each habitation he affixed a small piece of land as a garden. Then when the inhabitants were thinned out, Solomon had all the unsightly and worn out old habitations cleared away, and he built small habitations for the remaining poor, and he left patches of green around them, and he had the sweet smelling herbs of Arabia transplanted throughout Jerusalem, which was cleaned at certain periods, and the rocks from the White Islands* were burned and spread in all the thoroughfares of Jerusalem, so that the aroma from the sweet smelling herbs filled the city and was wafted for miles by the gentle breezes. And at certain distances the King had deep wells dug for the use of the people, and he had wains laden with clay from the interior and brought to Jerusalem and distributed to the poor to cleanse their linen and their persons and cure their eyelids from sores: and Solomon sent throughout Israel to get an account of the cattle and their breeds, the sheep and their breeds, the horses and camels and asses and their breeds, and from the King's treasury the poor or inferior beasts were bought, and the sheep and the oxen were slaughtered and given to the poor for food, and the asses and horses and camels of inferior breeds, they were taken out of the land and sold, and the money was given to the owners; but Solomon passed an edict that none of the inferior breeds should be bred again in Israel, so that in a few years the camels, the asses and horses were all of superior breeds, and remained so during the reign of Solomon.

Thus endeth the Sixteenth Chronicle of Solomon.

POEMS.

ENGLAND.

Richmond, Va., 1420 Main St., June 7, 1883.

There is no knowing; England's island home
May her protect a thousand years to come.
The sea that doth surround her is her shield :
Supremacy on it she ne'er must yield.

As every day and every year doth pass,
She is a mirror to mankind, a glass
In which her noble sentiments are shown.
Her ills are many, yet not overgrown.

The nation hath a strong, a logic mind,
A grand and quick perception. She is kind,
For Britain, it is full of art and skill,
Its rights for to defend hath power and will.

The education of the youthful brain,
Without distention or that fearful strain
That schools more westward urge with rapid force,
Till brains, distended, grow from bad to worse.

Her people are well fed, obey the laws ;
Her people are well clothed, and they have cause
For great rejoicing; never on the earth
Hath there been such an empire, such a girth

From truth and honor and their sterling worth:
For they are taught true principles from birth.
The time will come when England won't endure
The law that wrongs her—primogeniture

Will be cast from her. Debts then must be paid.
The nobles be more strict how debts are made.
The game laws gone, progressive statute books,
Then workingmen with gun and line and hooks,

So that they do not trespass, will be free
As ermined kings or the nobility.
A pheasant or a partridge or a snipe,
Will then be free from the baronial gripe.

If true refinement comes from noble birth,
Or from truth and honor, that social worth
That Britain loves, her children must progress.
And show mankind their sterling loveliness.

She is not perfect ; nations never were;
But all her offspring ever will revere,
Whether in Canada or Hindostan,
Or in Australia, every single man

Whose father or whose grandfather did come
From merry England—from that island home—
Revere her still, and form in every land
Sons of St. George, a firm, united band.

How many heroes doth her history show
Cut off by tyrants with a murderous blow?
Queen Boadicea, in her island home,
Conquered the legions of imperial Rome.

Caractacus, who for full twenty years
Filled many a Roman matron's eyes with tears,
Was filled with wonder at grand scenes in Rome,
That Cæsar envied him his cot at home.

King Alfred's memory ever will remain,
His noble laws, his life without a stain,
His laws the pedestal, Moses wrote the dome.
While Pandects famous from Justinian come.

King Harold he was brave, yea, very brave ;
And fought the Norman, who did soon enslave
The Saxons and the Danes by cruel laws.
From England's lion William drew the claws.

Yet Hareward brave and famous Robin Hood
Fought bravely on for fallen England's good,
But did not much advance; at length her speed
Accelerated at famous Runnymede.

From this time on till Cromwell ruled the land,
Destroyed the nobles' castles with his band,
And gave those principles the Pilgrims taught
To Yankee land from dear old England brought.

In later days, Cleve, Hethrington, Carlyle,
Taught moral truths. The nation now can smile.
Paine's Rights of Man, his book of common sense,
His agrarian justice recompense

For many years of sorrow. He set free
The colonies from Britain. Liberty
He taught mankind. Yea, in every page
His sterling sentiments did advance the age.

Now common schools, mechanics' institutes
Which guide the young idea as it shoots;
And household suffrage vote for men who rule
One-third of all the earth; therefore, no fool

Can lead the House of Commons, talent must,
Whether from plebeian ranks or upper crust:
Another decade, every one can write
Will vote in England, claim it as his right.

Then will old England be a merry band,
And with her offspring nations hand in hand,
Feel free and happy in her island home,
Waiting for the Millenium to come.

I AM READING SHAKSPEARE.

Written, Walnut Street, Chattanooga, Tenn., March 12th, 1882.

I am reading Shakspeare. He speaks of eyes,
  Describes their loveliness in language clear.
He says the stars to him are glimmering toys
  Beside the lustre of eyes to him most dear.

I am reading Shakspeare. He speaks of lips,
  No twanging bow hath such lovely arches,
There's naught more happy than the bee who sips
  The honey from them as it daily parches.

I am reading Shakspeare. He speaks of brows
  High and commanding as a tower of strength,
A power of grandeur as it daily grows,
  Broad as the ocean, as mountain high in length.

I am reading Shakspeare. He speaks of hair,
  Red, rich and golden, or of flaxen hue;
Of jetty hues with ravens' wings compare,
  In trailing masses, which are beauty's due.

He writes of brain, of grand, stupendous brain,
  Of human folly and of idiot minds,
Of thoughts which flow from tongues like showers of rain,
  Of love that is the strongest cord which binds.

He writes of death, the silence of the grave,
  Of cowardice, deceit and rage in man,
Of the great power of eloquence to save;
  Falseness in women who coquettish plan.

He speaks with all the eloquence of grace
  Of beauties who unrivalled stood in fame.
He makes a villain show a virtuous face,
  Who blackens deep with mire the fairest name.

He talks of base submission. kingly pride,
    Of fawning sycophants. of patriots brave,
Of those who o'er mankind would roughshod ride, .
    Of those would rather die than be a slave.

He paints the daisy as the meekest flower,
    He paints the rose as emblem of true love,
He elevates the lily with a dower
    Pure as the snowdrop, gentle as the dove.

He gives to passion wild a power and strength
    Fierce as the tiger's in its raging wrath,
Which like a fury springeth to its length,
    And maddened, foiled, its lips are fring'd with froth.

He paints the bird of beauty, (Paradise),
    He breaks the heart with some sad, plaintive tale,
Then portrays music in the charming voice
    Of that sweet thrilling bird. the nightingale.

Even his errors in geography,
    His setting sail on water for Milan
Are all forgotten in the melody
    Of this grand writer, world renownèd man.

There are a thousand errors in his tales,
    We these forget in reading language grand.
The lovely words mellifluous he inhales
    Who hath his marvelous writings near at hand.

He, like a spirit of the rosy morn,
    He, like a gleam of grandeur from the sun,
He, like no other mortal ever born,
    Can in wild mirth or sadness ever run.

We read the Bible and we seldom tire,
    Read Mirabeau and Toulman now and then,
Read Shelley o'er and o'er with new desire,
    And read Lord Byron with his caustic pen.

We read the logic of the famous Watts,
  The tried philosophy of Bacon read,
Read of astronomy and sunny spots
  Which fly off tangent brand new worlds to breed.

Of Milton who in writing was so grand,
  Of Pope and Addison and exquisite Steele,
Of dark skinned Homer from the sunlit land,
  Where the great river Nile slips from the reel.

Histories we read of England, France and Spain,
  Of Italy and Persia, Greece and Rome,
Gibbon's Decline and Fall, his type doth reign.
  Puts Allison and Napier at the dome.

We read of Buddha and Confucius,
  The great Xahada, Zeus, and of Christ,
Arab Mahomet, and we do discuss
  The different creeds the Priests do on us foist

Of hell and heaven and the human soul,
  Of right and wrong and of free will in man;
Read of the far off regions near the pole,
  They have no creed—dame Nature is their plan.

They need no garments, climate's balmy, warm,
  They need no dwellings, sleep beneath the trees,
Their freshness always is a perfect charm,
  Sans clothing, they are fragrant with the breeze.

They have no churches, buildings, fence or barn,
  The products of their country are for all;
Of them and Central Africans we learn,
  Who happiest are on this terrestrial ball.

We read the poets, Goethe, Schiller, Moore,
  Cowper, Alice Carey, Jean Ingelow,
Their streams of poesy glide forevermore,
  In rivulets of gold and silver flow.

How many novels in our time we've read,
  Rienzi, Scottish Chiefs and Ivanhoe,
Of Pompeii the City of the Dead,
  The great calamity, bright Italia's woe.

We read of wars by Semiramis bold,
  Nebuchdanezzar of Assyria read,
Of Jewish wars in Canaan we are told,
  Of Zenghis Khan which makes the heart to bleed.

Of Tamerlane, of Bajazet the Turk,
  Both Asiatic in their language true,
These wholesale murderers like to Hare and Burke,
  In Hades all will get their meed and due.

The wars of Cæsar and Hannibal we've read,
  Of great Napoleon that brave monster mind
For whom a hundred different nations bled,
  To rule the race he would have made all blind.

We have read the history of great Charlemagne,
  Of our own Alfred, also called the Great,
Of the great conquering Bastard who did reign
  O'er conquered England.   Sad was Harold's fate.

We read of great inventors, Arkwright, Watt,
  Of the great telegrapher, famous Morse,
Columbus, Galileo not forgot,
  Of Cleopatra filled with sad remorse.

Of Scythians and of Amazons we read,
  Of giants who did live in days of yore,
Of those two mothers to Solomon did plead,
  The false one's heart was cold unto the core.

We read of famed Zenobia, warlike queen,
  Who fought the Romans bravely for a while
Until their armies swiftly did careen,
  And took Zenobia in their snaring coil.

We read of authors in the days of yore,
   Moses, Isaiah, David, Solomon,
Plato and Socrates, a hundred more,
   Who from this earth in ancient times were gone.

But none were Shakspeare, he doth stand alone,
   Grand in blank verse and ocular in rhyme,
Tragic or comic, yet a moral zone
   Will e'er surround him till the end of time.

AN ANGEL'S VISIT.

Richmond, Va., March 29, 1883.

An angel came here with his beautiful wings,
   He sat himself down on my feathery bed,
And said unto me the most exquisite things,
   These were some of the words that the angel said:

"I will take thee up to the heavenly throne
   And introduce thee to the angelic throng,
Thy name to them, not entirely unknown,
   They love you as one of the Princes of Song."

On ladders of glory we soared up on high,
   'Till the arch of a rainbow was far down below,
And that which we see as a perfect blue sky
   Was transparent pure ether, whiter than snow.

A gateway of diamonds came to our view,
   The hedge rows were emerald wire as a screen.
To the high arch of heaven the angel he flew,
   And took me where never a mortal had been.

Oh what an expanse—most bewildering sight,
　　There were hundreds of millions whose promenade
Made gorgeous the glory with scintillas of light,
　　While a myriad of golden harps were played.

We came to the floor, such an exquisite floor,
　　Where a carpet pure white was bordered with green,
Then he opened a sapphire and emerald door,
　　Thousands on thousands of dancers were seen.

Cachucha, Mazurka, the Polka or Glide,
　　Or the waltzes we have at dances on earth
Are naught, for the angels with seraphic pride,
　　Danced to harps that were golden of heavenly birth.

I had a lovely partner with bright blue eyes
　　And a perfect mass of rich golden hair,
Her eyes they were purer than Italy's skies.
　　Few on this earth with her beauty compare.

And as we whirled round in the mazy dance,
　　And I encircling her waist with my hand,
My heart it beat quickly she did so entrance.
　　My senses I could not longer command.

To a seat we wandered, 'twas pearly white,
　　And I still basked in the light of her eyes ;
The earth I forgot in my spirit's new flight,
　　So entrancing, so angelic the joys.

Then I slept as I sat by the angel's side,
　　And I dreamed that I had received a new birth.
When lo I awoke with pleasure and pride
　　I found myself on this beautiful earth.

THE BEAUTIFUL SPRING.

Written, 1429 Main Street, Richmond, Va., May 3d, 1883.

———

'Tis an exquisite thing for a poet to sing
Of the caroling birds and the beautiful spring.
Our praise is due to the poet to-day
Who can sweetly before his readers lay
A description of flowers that come in spring:
'Tis delicious to hear such a poet sing.

He sings of the beautiful realms of light,
Of the foliage green so pleasant to sight,
And if he should sing of the glorious stars,
Or of fairies who float in their aerial cars,
Then it is a delightful, glorious thing,
In glowing sweet language to hear him sing.

When the poet doth sing of the human race
With wonderful language and perfect grace,
And showeth how grand and perfect the brain
That proceeds from the tiniest germ or grain,
'Tis then in language sublime he can sing
That the mind of man o'er the world is king.

POVERTY.

Written, Cleveland Infirmary, February 21st, 1882.

Oh ! poverty thou art the sting destroys
All source of tenderness, the very springs
Of all affection; it grinds the human heart
To the minutest atoms, and there leaves
A sanded desert, as Sahara is ;
In poverty the mother leaves her babe
Upon the steps of some rich burgher's door,
Hides the hard crust from her dear former love,
All pity hid by the fierce gnawing pains
That makes her wary for a mouldy crust.
When poverty comes home, the cottage door
Is closed against each neighbor.   As a slave
The strong man soon becomes.   Obsequious
And bending down unto the very dust,
He begs for orts the tradesman throws his dog.
If he doth labor they so cheapen it
He cannot for his family provide.
When sickness coming on for want of food.
He's taken to the poor-house hospital.

THE BULLS AND THE BEARS' BLACK MONDAY.

Written December 10th, 1869.

The Bulls and the Bears were struggling for gold,
Regardless of wrongs, for their hearts were cold.
And although grim Death in his easy chair,
Was *beckoning* for some who were gambling there.
With his ghastly mouth and *unsocketed* eyes,
While bony hands waved off the *pestering* flies,
Hearts swelled, and some broke in the terrible fight,
Death smiled till he grinned, and thought it all right.

The suicide gambled his millions away ;
Children tenderly reared are beggars to-day.
While those who had millions and gambled to swell
Their wealth and their crimes, are favorites of Hell.
And the Devil who dwells in that pleasant abode,
Will give them their sulphur, load upon load,
Will set Imps who are hungry to gnaw at their hearts,
And canker worms thrust in the scattered parts,
Until struggling with anguish, with pain untold,
They shriek out *damnation* unto the gold.

Note all the misery, the anguish, the care,
These gamblers produced, and quickly prepare
Statistics of all, and a balance sheet :
Then whene'er they are met, let the millions greet
Them with a deafening, deep groan of scorn,
Till writhing, they wish they had ne'er been born.
As Death twirls his claws in their clammy hair,
As they fix on him eyes with unearthly glare,
Let then reams of greenbacks and bonds be rolled
Up before their eyes as they clutch for gold.

Our *administration* should bring in a bill
Would on gamblers act like a mercury pill,
And make a just law all the nation would sign,
A *government* note should be equal to coin.*
All other banks should fork over and pay
The *rate* of the current *premium* the day
That the bill itself became law of the land,
On all notes they had issued or had on hand.
But if they redeemed hereafter in gold,
As such let their future issue be sold.
Then would Government stand in the world's esteem
Very high, and their notes in gold redeem.

TO THE LOVELY POET OF MACON.

Written, Friday, January 23d, 1880.

I send a friendly greeting and respect,
Whether thy spirit unto heaven hath gone,
On golden thrones to sit to take thy rest,
As floating by the stars in milky way,
Or still at Macon, this much will I say,
You seem the glorious essence of a soul
That would love to be wafted beyond this earth's control.

Violets have odor like the sweetest song,
And lilies have a purity like thee.
The passion flower, if that it had a tongue,
Would sing thy praises ; the industrious bee
Would gather golden honey from thy lips,
Regaling each on nectar as each sips ;
And I a stranger who thy Deluge saw,
A piece of lovely language without flaw.

Would love to know the author. Yet thy name
To me is yet unknown. And I,
Though longing to bask in the burning flame
That glistens in and sparkles in thine eye,
I trust again to see thy volume once,
That I the rest may read ; though but a dunce,
I trust my wit thy purity conceives ;
Although thou art a flower, hid 'neath the choicest
    leaves.

I heard a daisy talking to a rose,
I fear it did forget its modesty,
It said " thou art so fragrant, how choice thy blows.
How well thou art protected. What a joy
Springs from the admiration you receive."
The rose it answered, " Daisy, do not grieve,
Perhaps the maker of the flowers knew best,
Therefore pray be contented. Daisy strive to rest."

I heard a nightingale in evening's shade
Say as it sat upon a lonely tree,
" Behold the peacock, 'tis gorgeously arrayed,
How plain the colors nature gave to me."
The peacock heard it as it sat at rest,
And to the nightingale said, " He knows best
Who gave to me fine colors for my tail,
But made you queen of song, sweet lovely nightingale."

I wish I knew thee, if thou art on earth,
Thy countenance is charming and thine eye
Looks like a seraph's of pure heavenly birth,
Just like the glorious twinklers in the sky ;
Jean Ingelow in language is so choice,
That as a poetess few can her excel :
Shelley so sensitive with poetic voice
Doth sound delicious tocsins for mankind's reveille.

You like the pink, camilia, pansies fair,
Do purity and beauty so combine,

That like the parting of thy lovely hair,
Sheweth thy brow commanding, where beauty is divine;
There is a gentleness, a prayerful tone
In all thy loving language, delicate ;
The fervor of thy poesy is thy own,
And thy forms of beauty thou doth thyself create.

I am a prisoner, and the down-east sky
Seems 'though 'twere falling, laden down with snow
The blustering winds from Boreas do fly,
In furious wild tornadoes they do blow ;
The rivers are surcharged and o'er each field
(Which in the summer glorious crops will yield),
Show that it is stormy winter.   Yet my mind
To estimate thy beauteous language is inclined.

Strong bars of iron are 'tween you and I,
Yet there is a tiny opening in the cloud,
A spec within the distance, I will try
To place my discontent beneath a shroud.
The time will surely come I shall be free,
Then down to Georgia I will try to come,
And seek to find a personal pronoun, Thee,
And trust I shall be welcome to thy Southern home.

SULTAN OF BAGDAD'S DAUGHTER.

Written at Youngstown, Ohio, December 7, 1883.

About ten centuries ago,
In old, golden, glorious Bagdad,
Lived a sultan in such splendor,
That Aladdin's fairy garden,
With its trees with jewels laden,
Was a poor caravansary
Beside his gem and gold clad city,
In which with his starlike daughter,
Lived the Sultan of old Bagdad.
You have seen black Italian eyes
Twinkling like the star of morning,
Or the brighter one of evening;
Have seen all the merry twinkles
That will chain your heart forever.
Such eyes were the eyes of Lutee,
The glorious vision that on earth,
Somewhat east of old Judea,
Was proclaimed the starlike daughter
Of the Sultan of old Bagdad.
And her lips were wreathéd smiles
The sweet lower one a cherry,
While the dimples in her chin,
In her cheek and near her elbows,
Like the bloom of ripened peaches,
And the palest pink of roses,
Just a little brunette tinted,
Showed a face of eastern beauty;
Smote the heart of each beholder
With true love and wild amazement
For the Sultan's lovely daughter.
She was tall and very stately,
A Venus and a trifle Juno,
And her choice attitude was such,

Whether walking or reclining,
That she crazed her tens of thousands,
As they all were driven insane
Gazing on that glorious vision
Of the daughter of the Sultan.
Glorious sunlight and the starlight,
Grand Zenobia-looking Lutee,
Daughter of th' most gorgeous Sultan
Ever reigned in glorious Bagdad.
In the rear of that grand palace
(Oft reclined this beauty sleeping,
Watched o'er by Syrian angels,
With their golden wings extended,
Fanning her with attar breezes),
Was a most perfect paradise,
A rich and cultivated garden,
Where the luscious fruit was ripening,
And the sweet aromatic shrubs,
Brought away from old Arabia,
Filled this choice garden with perfume,
In an arbor covered over
With passion flowers, lovely roses,
With woodbines and honeysuckles,
While bushes of sweet eglantine,
Beds of sweetest mignonette,
And the loveliest beds of pansies,
Many colored choice verbenas,
With tulips that were rich and rare,
Pinks, sweetwilliams, pretty daisies,
Cockscombs and deep purple violets,
That their perfume saturated
Every spot within the garden,
In the rear of that grand palace,
Where did dwell the starlike daughter
Of the Sultan of old Bagdad.
Once Lutee walked outside the city,
Covered with a silken sunshade
In the hand of a young maiden,

With two eunuchs from the palace.
On a stone near to a village
Just three miles from ancient Bagdad,
Sat a man with ragged raiment,
But of an especial grandeur,
With a mien was quite majestic,
Fine proportioned, thews of iron,
Beautiful as Greek Adonis,
A perfect match for Hercules.
He had a manly, well-toned voice,
With eyes of perfect polished jet,
Ringlets black as wing of raven,
Grander in this glorious figure
Than the brave Grecian Diomede;
His teeth a perfect row of pearls,
And the music of his language,
Like the harp tones of Apollo,
Or the words which angels whisper,
Were commanding, soft, or gentle,
Or plaintive as a minor tone ;
And his limbs in fine proportion,
Like young Apollo Belvidere.
Such as gods on Mount Olympus
Might fairly worship and admire.
Lutee, the daughter of the Sultan,
Gazed upon his wondrous beauty.
Then seated at a little distance,
Did inquire with gentle words
About his country and his lineage,
Asked if he were a son of Jove.
Then he knelt beside the maiden,
Forgot about his ragged vestments,
Told a younger treacherous cousin,
Won by gold the strange affection
Of a warlike guilty people;
How he fought for days and days,
Until by twenty-four surrounded.
They called upon him to surrender, .

But with his axe and scimetar
He cleft his way right through them all,
Then mounted on an Arab charger,
Flew towards the Sultan's frontier,
Hoping for better times to come.
Was he hungry? was he thirsty?
Yes. Omar, flee on wings of wind,
Bring provisions, wine and water,
So that we may regale the stranger;
Othman, fly, and from the wardrobe
Of my regal, royal father;
Bring a splendid robe of purple.
They soon returning, Cartha feasted,
Washed in water, drank his wine,
Threw his outer garment from him,
Robed himself in purple splendor;
Then upon his Arab war-horse,
Follow'd by Lutee on a palfrey,
Which another eunuch brought her,
Then entered into glorious Bagdad;
Sought the Sultan in his palace,
And received especial favor,
Cartha the grandest new apparel;
Then he talked and told to Lutee
The same melting, loving story,
And she listened to his language
As she'd listen to an angel
Fresh from heaven's bright paradise.
And her father told Prince Cartha
That he would find him an army
So he could return again
And win the crown from the usurper.
But the troops of Calione,
Fearing lest their noble king
Should reward their treacherous conduct
With the bowstring or the axe,
Fought with unexampled fury,
Day by day, and each army

That the traitor's brother led,
Also that led by Calione,
Seemed like gods, such was their valor.
But the Sultan sent Abdala
With another fifty thousand,
And they went to winter quarters,
For the cold in western Medea
From the northern blasts set in.
Midway between the troops and Bagdad,
Came the grand majestic Cartha,
Came the loving Bagdad princess,
And the Sultan in his grandeur.
They waited for the sunny spring.
Cartha pleaded, pleaded daily,
For her hand and to be wedded,
And she listened to his loving,
Loving language as he pleaded,
For 'tis given to Persians only
And those who use the Arab tongue
To paint the lovely lily whiter,
And gild gold refined in song,
By the pathos of their language;
But the Sultan old and wiser,
Said you will lose naught by waiting,
Bade Cartha move his troops on soon.
He came upon Arphar, the traitor,
And slew him with his scimetar,
Then the army did surrender,
And the lovely Sultan's daughter
Did become the bride of Cartha.
Cartha he was tender hearted,
And forgave his rebel soldiers,
He forgave them every one.
So within a splendid palace
Most magnificent with grandeur,
Dwelt King Cartha and fair Lutee;
And the Sultan was made happy,
By the visits from his daughter.

She would sing such plaintive songs,
Just as once did Judah's daughters
As they passed o'er the Euphrates,
About the lovely running rivers,
About the shepherds tending sheep;
Sang about the twining roses,
Of the pansies and the daisies,
Sang of the lovely passion flower,
Sang about the loves of angels,
Of the passions of immortals;
Sang of the virtues of a child,
Of mignonette so aromatic,
Of the grand Damascus roses,
Of love within the human heart,
Of lovely birds of paradise,
Of nightingales, the queens of song,
Then she would sing of human nature,
Of its overflowing goodness,
And sang about the coming time,
When the earth would see millenium.
She, her husband and her father,
Were buried in a grand mausoleum
In the city of old Bagdad.